ADAPTING TO
CLIMATE CHANGE

ADAPTING TO
CLIMATE CHANGE

BY AMANDA LANSER

CONTENT CONSULTANT
ANKUR DESAI
ASSOCIATE PROFESSOR
ATMOSPHERIC AND OCEANIC SCIENCES
UNIVERSITY OF WISCONSIN–MADISON

Essential Library

An Imprint of Abdo Publishing | www.abdopublishing.com

www.abdopublishing.com

Published by Abdo Publishing, a division of ABDO, PO Box 398166, Minneapolis, Minnesota 55439. Copyright © 2015 by Abdo Consulting Group, Inc. International copyrights reserved in all countries. No part of this book may be reproduced in any form without written permission from the publisher. Essential Library™ is a trademark and logo of Abdo Publishing.

Printed in the United States of America, North Mankato, Minnesota
032014
092014

Cover Photo: iStock/Thinkstock
Interior Photos: iStock/Thinkstock, 2; U.S. Air Force, Master Sgt. Mark C. Olsen/AP Images, 6; NOAA/AP Images, 10; Craig Ruttle/AP Images, 12; Thinkstock, 16, 57, 68; Dorling Kindersley RF/Thinkstock, 19; Imaginechina/AP Images, 24, 46; Mel Evans/AP Images, 29; Diane Cook and Len Jenshel/National Geographic/Getty Images, 31; Delme Thomas Photography/Thinkstock, 34; Red Line Editorial, 37, 54; Ian Barrett, CP/AP Images, 44; Arno Burgi/picture-alliance/dpa/AP Images, 52; Ethan Daniels/Shutterstock Images, 58; Rex Features/AP Images, 61; Rebecca Blackwell/AP Images, 70; NOAA, 73; The Las Cruces Sun-News, Shari Vialpando-Hill/AP Images, 79; Post-Tribune, Jerry Schultheiss/AP Images, 82; Mark Wragg/Thinkstock, 84; David Moir/Reuters/Corbis, 89; Marcel Jancovic/Shutterstock Images, 94

Editor: Melissa York
Series Designer: Becky Daum

Library of Congress Control Number: 2014932559

Cataloging-in-Publication Data

Lanser, Amanda.
 Adapting to climate change / Amanda Lanser.
   p. cm. -- (Essential issues)
Includes bibliographical references and index.
ISBN 978-1-62403-416-9
1. Climatic changes--Social aspects--Juvenile literature. 2. Climate change--Juvenile literature.   I. Title.
363.6--dc23

2014932559

CONTENTS

CHAPTER 1

**CLIMATE CHANGE
OR WILD WEATHER?**   6

CHAPTER 2

**THE SCIENCE OF
CLIMATE CHANGE**   16

CHAPTER 3

**WHAT DOES IT
MEAN TO ADAPT?**   24

CHAPTER 4

**A BIT OF CLIMATE
CHANGE HISTORY**   34

CHAPTER 5

FUELING THE FUTURE   46

CHAPTER 6

CHANGING OCEANS   58

CHAPTER 7

**HEAT, DROUGHTS,
AND FLOODS**   70

CHAPTER 8

CAN WE FIX THE FUTURE?   84

Timeline   96
Essential Facts   100
Glossary   102
Additional Resources   104
Source Notes   106
Index   110
About the Author   112

CHAPTER
ONE

CLIMATE CHANGE OR WILD WEATHER?

Engineer Mike McDonald decided to stay put at his Union Beach, New Jersey, home on the night of October 29, 2012. He was not intimidated by the forecasts of local and national meteorologists, who warned New Jersey residents that a powerful storm named Sandy was heading their way. McDonald had ridden out severe weather in the past. He didn't think this storm would be any different.

But Sandy was different. Record high tides combined with a powerful storm surge to produce intense coastal flooding. Seawater started seeping through cracks in McDonald's front door. Then, it suddenly gushed through the front window and burst through the entryway. McDonald, an experienced diver, realized unless he got out fast, he would be trapped in

The storm Sandy caused many coastal homes to flood.

his flooded home. He ran upstairs, wrestled into his wetsuit, and grabbed a boogie board to help himself stay afloat. McDonald escaped through a dining room window into the black, churning water. His adventure was only beginning.

McDonald was not alone in the water. Debris threatened to catch his ankles and pull him under. McDonald half-swam and half-climbed through the floodwater and debris. Eventually, he pulled himself up onto the porch of Walter Anderson's home five blocks from his own. Anderson gave McDonald some dry clothes and water. Later, Union Beach police officers brought McDonald to a school serving as a storm shelter.

McDonald's home was destroyed by the storm. When asked if he would try to stay in his old neighborhood, McDonald was emphatic. "I will not rebuild," he said.[1] Approximately 650,000 homes were destroyed by Sandy.[2] In the aftermath, scientists and journalists were asking the same question: Did climate change cause Sandy?

Anatomy of a Storm

No one can refute Sandy was a severe storm. When it hit the mid-Atlantic states of the United States,

Sandy was considered a post-tropical cyclone. Since 2010, the National Weather Service has used the term *post-tropical cyclone* for storms that were once, but are no longer, hurricanes.

Nevertheless, when it collided with the East Coast, Sandy caused record-setting storm conditions. Tropical storm–force winds from the storm spanned nearly 1,000 miles (1,600 km) from Maine to South Carolina. A satellite image of Sandy indicated the entire storm covered a whopping 1.8 million square miles (4.7 million sq km).[3] Wind speeds at landfall clocked in at around 80 miles per hour (130 kph), just over the threshold required for a storm to be considered a hurricane.[4]

The storm also caused significant damage. Storm surge was the primary culprit. Storm surge is the abnormal rise in sea level due to an intense storm. Scientists measure it by finding the difference between the level of the sea during a storm and

A COSTLY STORM

At more than $50 billion in damages, Sandy was the sixth-costliest cyclone to hit the United States since 1900, adjusted for inflation.[5] At least 650,000 homes were destroyed and 8.5 million people lost power.[6] Sandy was also the most deadly hurricane-like storm since Hurricane Katrina in 2005. The storm caused 147 deaths, including 48 in New York, 12 in New Jersey, 5 in Connecticut, 2 in Virginia, 2 in Pennsylvania, and 1 each in New Hampshire, West Virginia, and Maryland.[7]

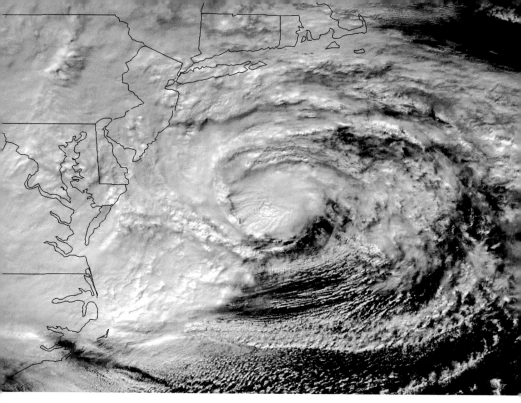
Sandy affected a wide area on the East Coast.

the level of the sea surface during normal conditions. Sandy happened to hit the United States during some of the highest recorded tides of the year, which meant sea levels were already quite high. Tide gauges measured water levels as high as eight feet (2.4 m) above ground level during Sandy.[8]

The storm surge wreaked havoc on New York City and the Jersey Shore. Seawater flooded subway tunnels in Manhattan and the runways at La Guardia and Kennedy airports. Flooding cost the New Jersey Transit System $400 million.[9] Houses along the shores on Staten

Island and New Jersey were swept off their foundations, while seawater carried cars and boats inland. In communities where homes suffered less damage, home owners still faced months of power outages, as much of the utility infrastructure in the area was damaged or destroyed.

Did Climate Change Cause Sandy?

After Sandy, President Barack Obama called for a federal task force to investigate how to reduce the impact of future storms and recommend ways to rebuild areas damaged by Sandy. The task force came up with dozens of suggestions, among them making new construction more hurricane-resistant and cell phone service more impenetrable to storm and water damage. Another recommendation? Take climate change into account in future storm preparations.

Most scientists agree global warming and resulting climate change do not cause individual storms like Sandy. However, experts have found strong evidence global warming can change global weather conditions. That's because when Earth's temperature increases, ocean waters get warmer and the atmosphere becomes more humid. Wind shear, or the sudden shift in wind

Some people needed to be rescued from their homes following the superstorm.

speed and direction, also increases. These are factors that may fuel extreme weather.

A 2013 report issued by the Intergovernmental Panel on Climate Change (IPCC) found that though it was unlikely intense storms would increase in the first half of the 2000s, it was "more likely than not" that storm intensity would increase in the latter half of the century.[10] MIT scientist Kerry Emanuel has found evidence hurricane intensity could increase by 45 percent globally by 2100.[11] However, both Emanuel and the IPCC state their predictions are not set in stone. Some models show an increase in intensity, while others have mixed results.

With more intense storms would come more intense storm surges. Though tides—controlled by the moon—play a role in the severity of storm surges, rising sea levels due to global warming could also make storm surges more powerful. Warmer ocean temperatures cause thermal expansion of the ocean because warmer water has a low density. Glacial ice in the Arctic starts melting as the planet warms. Thermal expansion of the oceans and ice melt explain approximately 75 percent of the rise in global sea levels.[12] The IPCC projects that by 2100, sea levels around the globe could rise two to seven feet (0.6 to 2 m) higher than they are now. Seven feet (2 m) is only one foot (0.3 m) shy of the eight-foot (2.4 m) storm surge that caused the destruction during Sandy.[13]

While scientists are reluctant to place direct blame for Sandy on climate change, they currently accept climate change will contribute to more intense storms in the future. As the director of the Institute on the Environment at the University of Minnesota, Jonathan Foley, tweeted, "Would this kind of storm happen without climate change? Yes. Fueled by many factors. Is [the] storm stronger because of climate change? Yes."[14]

Climate Change and Us

Sandy and the resulting damage are just one example of how scientists predict climate change will affect the planet. As the global temperature rises, changes in sea level and extreme weather will have an impact on the lives of people all over the world. Rising temperatures are also predicted to cause a shift in when the seasons begin and end as well as a change in the ranges where animals and plants live. A warmer, moister planet may also increase instances of heat-related illness around the globe, as well as enlarging the range of tropical diseases.

So why should people care about climate change? In 2013, 97 percent of climate change scientists and researchers agreed not only that climate change is occurring, but that human activity is causing a lot of it.[15] That's why, in addition to seeking methods to slow and possibly stop human-caused climate change, called mitigation, many scientists are researching ways humans can adapt to climate change and perhaps reduce the effect climate change will have on humans in the future. This may mean finding ways to adapt to rising sea levels or earlier springs and later falls, or it may require humans to adapt their behaviors to climate change, for example, by decreasing energy use during heat waves.

While scientists are researching new, innovative ways to adapt to climate change, political leaders are still debating whether humans need to act. Regardless of changes to political policy that may or may not occur in the United States and around the globe, innovators are working on ways to help humans continue living comfortably on a planet that is increasingly warmer and more extreme.

GRADUAL IMPACTS

Not all climate change impacts are extreme. Many will be gradual and take years to develop. Though these changes may be slow, they will be serious. For example, in the United States, climate change is causing changes in the life cycles of birds. Warmer springs are causing some bird species to start nesting earlier in the year and begin their spring migration sooner. This can affect food sources and breeding habits. Other animals are finding their ranges are expanding farther north due to warmer temperatures while, at the same time, animals who call the northern climates home are seeing their ranges shrink. Though gradual, these changes can have a drastic effect on species population, perhaps even leading to extinction.

CHAPTER TWO

THE SCIENCE OF CLIMATE CHANGE

What do changes in temperature, an increase or decrease in precipitation, and changes in wind patterns that occur over several decades all have in common? They are all examples of climate change. Climate is the usual weather patterns in a region over time. The US Environmental Protection Agency (EPA) defines climate change as "any significant change in the measures of climate lasting for an extended period of time."[1] One important factor that contributes to climate change is global warming caused by an increase of greenhouse gases in the atmosphere. Scientists warn significant climate change will have a negative impact on the Earth and the millions of species that inhabit it, including humans.

Greenhouse gases from factories and industry are one contributor to climate change.

Greenhouse Gases and Global Warming

To understand how climate change occurs, it is necessary to understand the effects greenhouse gases have on the temperature of the Earth. The global temperature of the planet depends on the balance of energy entering Earth's atmosphere and energy leaving the atmosphere. Energy from the sun accounts for the energy entering Earth's atmosphere. Two main factors contribute to the energy that leaves Earth's atmosphere: the reflectivity of Earth's surface and changes in the greenhouse gases in the atmosphere. Not all of the sun's energy is absorbed by Earth's oceans, forests, and soils. Some of it is reflected back by light-colored surfaces, such as snow-covered fields or clouds. Liquid droplets in the

IT'S GETTING HOT IN HERE!

Though the decade experienced a relative pause in the increase in global temperature, the ten years between 2000 and 2010 were the warmest on record. In addition, the years 2005 and 2010 tied for the warmest year on record.[2] This change in global temperature has created some extreme changes. For example, in 2011 the summer low ice level in the Arctic was 1 million square miles (2.6 million sq km) below the average low ice levels between 1979 and 2000.[3] That's about the area of all the states east of the Mississippi River.

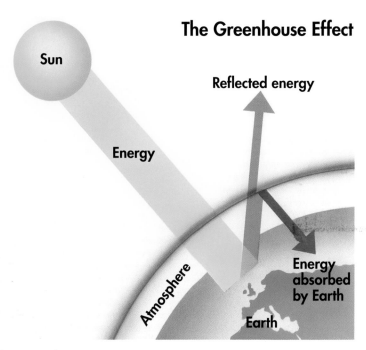

The Greenhouse Effect

Sun

Reflected energy

Energy

Atmosphere

Energy absorbed by Earth

Earth

Earth's atmosphere traps some energy so it can't escape to space. This heats the planet.

atmosphere can also reflect the sun's energy and let it leave Earth's atmosphere.

The balance of greenhouse gases present in the atmosphere also affects how much of the sun's energy stays in Earth's atmosphere. Greenhouse gases absorb energy from Earth that would otherwise escape into space. This causes Earth's temperature to increase. This phenomenon is called the greenhouse effect. There are four greenhouse gases that cause concern for climate change scientists: carbon dioxide, nitrous oxide, methane, and various fluorinated gases. Fluorinated gases include chemicals such as the hydrofluorocarbons (HFCs) used in industrial activity. The atmospheric levels of these greenhouse gases are considered anthropogenic, or influenced by humans. Greenhouse gases can stay in the atmosphere for decades.

When the energy gets absorbed, this causes the global temperature of Earth to increase. This rise in the average temperature of Earth is called global warming. Scientific evidence shows the increase in greenhouse gases in the atmosphere is the primary cause of global

MEET THE GREENHOUSE GASES

Carbon dioxide, methane, nitrous oxide, and fluorinated gases are the four main anthropogenic greenhouse gases found in the atmosphere. They also make up the majority of greenhouse gas emissions from the energy and other industries in the United States. Carbon dioxide made up 84 percent of all US greenhouse gas emissions in 2011. Carbon dioxide is released into the atmosphere when coal, oil, natural gas, trees, and solid waste are burned for energy.

Methane made up 9 percent of US emissions. Methane is released during agricultural production and by the decay of waste at landfills. Nitrous oxide made up 5 percent of emissions. Nitrous oxide is released into the atmosphere when coal, oil, and natural gas are burned for energy and during agricultural activities. Though fluorinated gases were only 2 percent of US emissions in 2011, they are very potent. A variety of industries release fluorinated gases into the atmosphere.[4]

warming. In the past 100 years, the global temperature of Earth has increased 1.4 degrees Fahrenheit (0.78°C).[5] Though that might not sound like much, even a slight change can cause dramatic changes in climate and weather.

THE GREENHOUSE EFFECT

The greenhouse effect is not necessarily a negative phenomenon. Without greenhouse gases, Earth would not be warm enough to sustain life. Scientific evidence suggests without the greenhouse effect, Earth's average surface temperature would only be approximately 0 degrees Fahrenheit (–18°C).[6]

If the global temperature of Earth rises enough, it may cause a variety of problems that will affect humans. Warmer global temperatures cause glacial ice to melt. When glaciers melt, the water that was trapped as ice flows into the oceans, raising global sea levels. Rising sea levels put coastal cities and towns at risk. Global warming may lead to droughts and flooding, which can destroy food crops, homes, and businesses.

What Causes Global Warming and Climate Change?

By collecting and analyzing evidence in tree rings, ice cores, pollen remains, and ocean sediments, scientists have learned what has caused Earth's climate to change over time. Before the Industrial Revolution, the period beginning in the late 1700s in which humans began burning fossil fuels for energy, natural phenomena could explain changes to the global climate. For example, changes in the amount of energy from the sun and volcanic eruptions can cause variations in global temperature. So can natural changes in the concentration of greenhouse gases in the atmosphere.

However, since the Industrial Revolution, and especially over the past 50 years, dramatic changes in greenhouse gas concentrations and global warming cannot be explained by natural causes alone. When fossil fuels such as coal and oil are burned for energy, they release carbon dioxide into the atmosphere. This adds to the concentration of greenhouse gases in the atmosphere, which in turn contributes to global warming. In fact,

WHERE DO EMISSIONS COME FROM?

Together, countries across the globe produce billions of metric tons of greenhouse gases every year. A variety of things contribute to that huge number. Energy usage accounted for the largest percentage of greenhouse gases in 2005, representing 73 percent of greenhouse gas emissions. Agriculture was next, accounting for 16 to 17 percent of emissions.[7]

carbon dioxide levels in the atmosphere are higher now than they have been in the last 800,000 years.[8]

As humans continue burning fossil fuels for energy, transportation, and other needs, the global temperature will continue rising. To continue on the same path humans have for the past century, it will be necessary to adapt to more frequent climate change impacts, including rising sea levels, changes to the growing season, and severe weather. Scientists are already working on some of these adaptations, while others are just the glimmer of someone's big idea.

CHAPTER
THREE

WHAT DOES IT MEAN TO ADAPT?

Research conducted by both government and private sector scientists has established that climate change is happening and human activity is a contributing factor. Scientists project much of the carbon dioxide presently in the atmosphere may remain there for at least 100 years.[1] Even if greenhouse gas emissions were to drastically decrease in the near future, the effects of global warming and climate change would continue affecting the Earth—and humankind. That is why some level of adaptation to the effects of climate change will be inevitable.

What Is Adapting to Climate Change?

Some climate scientists focus their efforts on how to mitigate climate change, while others look for ways for humans to adapt to living with the effects of climate change. Climate change adaptation is the effort society

Part of adapting to climate change may include changing how or where we grow crops.

makes to adjust to or prepare for climate change. The goal of climate change adaptation is to protect the resources that are most important to modern human life, including food crops, water, and energy resources.

Adapting to climate change involves a wide range of human activities. Protecting food and water resources is a primary concern. As extreme weather causes severe drought in some places and flooding in others, it may become necessary to develop crops that are tolerant of drought, flooding, and heat. Similarly, water resources will require protection to guarantee there is enough drinkable water.

Other adaptations may affect where and how humans live. Those living on or near the coasts may need to relocate or build their homes to withstand rising sea levels. Inland residents may build their homes to withstand more extreme storms. People could be required to increase their energy efficiency to offset US or global energy use to help mitigate global warming. Modifying human behavior will likely be important in future attempts to address climate change.

How Are Humans Adapting to Climate Change?

In the aftermath of Sandy, thousands of homeowners along the New York and New Jersey coastlines had to ask themselves whether they wanted to rebuild their seaside homes. Some chose to leave permanently, spurred by the rapidly rising cost of flood insurance. Those who chose to rebuild had to decide if they were going to build their homes as they were before the storm

ADAPTING AFTER SANDY

Homeowners are not the only ones adapting to climate change after Sandy. City officials and businesses in New York City are retrofitting their infrastructures to withstand future extreme weather. During Sandy, the power substation for Con Edison, the company that provides power to the city of Manhattan, flooded. The storm pushed water over the 11-foot (3.4 m) flood walls and flooded the station, causing a power failure. Now, Con Edison has installed new aluminum doors on its substations to prevent future flooding, as well as new waterproof equipment in its power stations that sit under the sidewalks of New York City.

Telecom company Verizon also had to make changes to its cable infrastructure. Sandy caused more damage to the company's cables than it had seen in 100 years. Verizon stores its copper telephone cables and fuel pump for its emergency generators in the subbasements of a building in Manhattan. Flooding destroyed the copper cables and rendered the emergency generator useless. Now, Verizon has changed all its copper cabling in the city to waterproof fiber-optic cables and encased its fuel pump in a room with a submarine door.

hit or adapt their design to take potential future storms into account. To avoid a large increase in flood insurance costs, some homeowners lifted their homes onto piles so they sat five or even ten feet (1.5 to 3 m) in the air, above the flood level of an event such as Sandy.

Elevating homes so they sit above the flood level is only one example of how humans are adapting to future climate change. Adapting to climate change happens on a small scale, such as homeowners taking future extreme weather into account in their home designs. Adapting also takes place on a large scale, such as changing government or international policy. Individuals, scientific organizations, governments, and international bodies are all

ADAPTING ANIMALS

Animals will need to adapt to climate change, too. Some species may migrate to new areas, while some bird species may change when and how they migrate. For example, the wood thrush, a species of songbird, migrates from forests in Canada to tropical forests in Central America each year. Though the species leaves Canada around the same time each year, it has changed the path it takes down to the tropics to avoid poor local weather conditions. Another study suggests mammal species may decrease in physical size as a result of global warming. That is what happened during a warming period 55 million years ago. Scientists project mammal body size may shrink because plants exposed to high carbon dioxide levels become less nutritious.

Some people choose not to rebuild after a flood or storm like Sandy.

working on projects to help humankind adapt to the effects of climate change.

What's the Holdup?

Though adapting to climate change is important, making such changes is challenging. It requires not only substantial financial resources but also the political and cultural will to change. For some, these costs outweigh the perceived benefit of adapting to climate change. Others debate the need for adaptation in the first place.

Making the necessary local, state, national, and international adaptations to climate change will be costly. The World Bank estimated in 2011 that adapting to a 3.6 degree Fahrenheit (2°C) increase in global temperature between 2010 and 2050 is likely to cost $70 billion to $100 billion per year.[2] That is more than the total gross domestic product (GDP) of many developing nations, though very low compared with the GDP of developed nations such as the United States and the United Kingdom. In fact, it is close to the same amount of money developed nations give in aid to developing countries.

Though economists have not analyzed what the national costs of climate change adaptation would

Architects are choosing green roofs for more buildings, an
example of a local adaptation to warmer temperatures.
These roofs bring down city temperatures.

be, they do predict the costs would unevenly affect different areas of the United States. For example, coastal communities will bear the brunt of rising sea levels, with price estimates as high as $210.8 billion between 2011 and 2100, or approximately $2.3 billion per year.[3] Adaptations made to protect national water supplies could cost up to $294.4 billion annually by 2095.[4]

State and local governments would need to bear some of the cost of climate change adaptations, too. For example, a statewide heat-warning system in California could cost the state $570,000 to set up and another similar sum every year to respond to the effects of heat-related illnesses.[5] In the Yakima Valley of the state of Washington, experts predict the costs of an improved irrigation system to guarantee water reaches crops would be $2.2 billion.[6]

Lack of political or cultural will to adapt to climate change also makes adapting more difficult. Politicians and individuals may be reluctant to make climate change adaptations now because the extremely negative impacts of a warmer planet are still in the future, as are the political and cultural benefits of adapting to climate change. Others do not believe widely accepted climate science and are making efforts to thwart climate change adaptation legislation.

Adapting to climate change is something in which everyone will need to participate. Individuals, organizations, the government, and international communities will need to work together to ensure everyone still has access to food, water, energy, and shelter as climate change takes effect. Though reaching consensus on what needs to be done can be difficult, most experts agree everyone needs to take action to adapt to the changing planet.

CITIES ADAPT

Municipalities can adapt to climate change by upgrading building codes and other policies to plan for future extreme weather. For example, cities may require new buildings to have extra insulation, a natural ventilation system, and window shading to reduce the energy needed to heat and cool the structures. Large cities may require buildings to install green roofs lush with plants. This would help lower the temperature in the city, thus requiring less energy to cool large buildings. Nationally, the United States could decentralize the national electric grid. In the case of extreme weather like Sandy, having many smaller grids may help some areas maintain power.

CHAPTER
FOUR

A BIT OF CLIMATE CHANGE HISTORY

Scientists have shown some degree of adapting to climate change will be necessary. But obstacles stand in the way of making some of these adaptations. Though climate change caused by natural factors is as old as Earth itself, the climate change recorded in the last 100 years cannot be attributed to natural causes alone. Humans have contributed to the concentration of greenhouse gases in the atmosphere, leading to global warming and climate change. While most scientists agree with that statement, there are some, including some policy makers, who deny humanity's impact on climate change. The debate between scientists and political activists has shaped how the United States and other nations have reacted to climate change.

Scientific evidence shows humans have contributed to current climate change since the Industrial Revolution.

Climate Change since the Industrial Revolution

Prior to the Industrial Revolution, most of Earth's climate change could be attributed to natural causes. During the Industrial Revolution, people began burning coal as energy and for use in transportation. New technologies developed during that time increased the concentrations of greenhouse gases in the atmosphere. In fact, experts have observed that since the Industrial Revolution, humans have increased the concentration of carbon dioxide in the atmosphere by 30 percent.[1]

Scientists started studying climate change in the 1800s. By the 1900s, a warming trend could be detected. By the century's end, the average global temperature had risen 1.08 degrees Fahrenheit (0.6°C). The temperature did not increase steadily from 1900 to 1999. Global temperatures actually decreased between 1940 and 1970. After 1970, however, temperatures rapidly increased. The decade of the 1990s had some of the highest global temperatures ever recorded.[2]

Meanwhile, greater national and international attention was being paid to global environmental problems. During the 1970s, the US government began

Average Global Temperature, 1800–2011

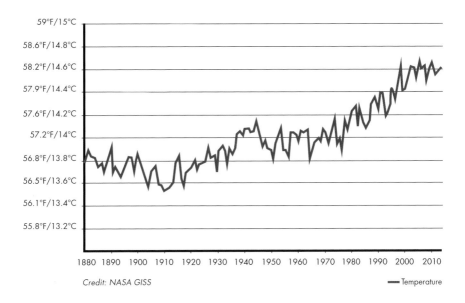

Credit: NASA GISS

— Temperature

recognizing the environment as a national issue. On December 2, 1970, President Richard Nixon established the Environmental Protection Agency in the wake of growing concern over pollution's effects on the air, water, and land in the United States. Seven years later, on October 1, President Jimmy Carter established the Department of Energy. It was tasked with researching and regulating energy development in the country, including nuclear energy and renewable energy. In the 1980s, President Ronald Reagan signed an international treaty called the Montreal Protocol that required signers to stop producing chemicals that depleted the ozone layer.

International bodies on climate change also started organizing. In February 1979, international organizations such as the World Meteorological Organization and the United Nations Environment Programme held the First World Climate Conference. The goal of the conference was to evaluate what scientists already knew about climate and how climate change might affect human populations. In 1988, the two organizations created the IPCC.

Under President George H. W. Bush, elected in 1988, the United States ratified the United Nations Framework Convention on Climate Change on October 13, 1992. The treaty is designed to prevent humans from contributing to future climate change. In the later years of the Bill Clinton administration (1993–2001), the United States worked on the Kyoto Protocol, a landmark agreement between developed nations to reduce greenhouse gas emissions. The United States signed the protocol in 1998; however, Congress never ratified it, so the United States was never required to reduce emissions under the agreement.

In 2005, during the presidency of George W. Bush, the provisions of the Kyoto Protocol took effect across the world without the United States participating. Though agreed on by 141 nations, scientists have begun worrying the Kyoto Protocol may not be making much of a dent in global greenhouse gas emissions because some of the world's largest producers of greenhouse gases, the United States and Russia, did not ratify it.

In May 2006, former vice president Al Gore released a documentary that would spark a new national conversation about climate change: *An Inconvenient Truth*. In it, he describes the dangers humans and the world will face as climate change intensifies in the future. A year later, the IPCC released a report considered the most "definitive" report on climate

WHY DIDN'T CONGRESS RATIFY THE KYOTO PROTOCOL?

Though the United States signed the Kyoto Protocol agreement in 1997, Congress never ratified it. At the time, there was little support for national legislative efforts to reduce greenhouse gas emissions. Representatives argued that reducing emissions would be costly. They were concerned that developing nations were exempt from reducing greenhouse gas emissions. Instead, the Senate unanimously passed the Byrd-Hagel resolution, which declared the "United States should not be a signatory to any protocol" regarding climate change.[4]

change science.[3] The report asserts not only that climate change is happening, but that humans have had a significant hand in the warming of Earth since the Industrial Revolution.

Not all people who saw the film or read the report believed the science, however. By the 1990s, people who were skeptical of climate change science had begun voicing their opinions. For example, in 1998, a group called the Global Climate Science Team created a plan to challenge the evidence from climate change science. The goal of the plan was to make sure people in the United States understood some of the nuances and uncertainties of climate change science. The Global Climate Science Team claimed climate change scientists were misrepresenting data and inflating the strength of the consensus among scientists that climate change was happening, which in turn misled the public.

Climate change skeptics quickly changed the nature of the climate change conversation. In 1998, the then-CEO of oil company ExxonMobil, Lee Raymond, grew convinced the science behind the Kyoto Protocol and climate change in general was incorrect. In fact, his company had lobbied against the ratification of the Kyoto Protocol in Congress. Around the same time *An*

Inconvenient Truth came out, an energy industry think tank released a number of ads challenging the science in climate change research. The main message of the ads was "Carbon dioxide. They call it pollution. We call it life."[5]

A few years later, the Heartland Institute, a conservative think tank, also contributed to the conversation. In 2009, it published a report concluding that though Earth's temperatures may be warming, human activity is not the cause. Instead, the report cited natural causes as the culprit behind climate change.

ATMOSPHERE OF SKEPTICISM

Americans' opinions on climate change and society's role in it have changed significantly over the years. In 2006, a poll found 47 percent of Americans believed solid evidence existed that Earth was warming and humans contributed to the rising temperature.[6] Just two years later, however, a Pew Research Center poll found a "sharp decline" in the number of Americans who believed global temperatures were rising. When the Pew Research Center broke down the data, it found Americans who identified politically as independents experienced the steepest decline,

from 75 percent in 2008 to 53 percent in 2009. In addition, the number of people who believed humans had an impact on global warming was down 11 percentage points to 36 percent.[7] In 2011, the number of Americans who believed there was solid evidence of human-caused climate change increased two percentage points from 2009 to 38 percent.[8] However, Sandy seems to have had a strong effect on public opinion. Polls taken after the storm found approximately 44 percent of adults believed Earth was warming due to human activity.[9]

Two years later, the group clarified its position: "We are not saying [human-caused] greenhouse gases (GHG) *cannot* produce some warming or have not in the past. Our conclusion is that the evidence shows they are not playing a substantial role."[10]

Climate change skeptics would change the shape of the national—and international—conversation on climate change and how the United States should adapt to the warming planet. Those who do not believe the climate is changing or changing enough to require action see little wisdom in investing in costly adaptation projects. The disagreement between scientists and skeptics makes it less likely policy makers will take action to assign funds for projects such as protecting national water supplies or improving crop irrigation.

A Political Challenge

In 2010, NASA released research that found the decade between 2000 and 2009 was the warmest ten years ever recorded.[11] The National Academy of Sciences also released a report asserting that climate change, caused by human activities, is affecting both natural ecosystems and human society. By that time, however, people who did not believe the climate change science were shaping the national discussion on climate change. The academy denounced the "political assaults" on climate change scientists by those skeptical of humanity's influence on Earth's warming temperature.[12]

Over the next two years, it became clear climate change policy was low on the list of priorities for legislators and the president. In 2011, the US Congress disbanded the House Committee on Global Warming, explaining that doing so not only reduced waste in government spending but also gave the responsibility of addressing climate change to scientists. During the 2012 presidential campaign, Democratic sitting president Barack Obama and Republican challenger Mitt Romney barely mentioned climate change. President Obama asserted in an August 2012 speech that climate change was "not a hoax" and the weather effects of climate change were "not a joke" but "a threat to our children's future," but he had failed to discuss it in his State of the

"Politicians and parts of the public may think climate change is still up for debate, but for nearly every scientist who knows the subject, the case is closed. . . . But just because the basics of climate science have been established doesn't mean we know everything about how fast the planet will warm—and what will happen when it does."[13]
—Bryan Walsh, writer and editor for TIME magazine, explaining the challenge of how to adapt to climate change

Worldwide, people are working to prevent climate change.

Union address eight months prior.[14] On the campaign trail, Romney directly challenged the idea that humans contributed to climate change. After President Obama was reelected, he started work on a plan to reduce the country's greenhouse gas emissions. The plan has a goal of reducing emissions by 17 percent by 2020.[15] To do so, President Obama needed to stretch legal interpretations of the Clean Air Act signed by President Nixon on December 31, 1970. In addition, in late 2013 President Obama appointed Dan Utech as his new energy and climate change adviser. Prior to accepting the position,

Utech helped create the administration's climate change agenda, including several adaptations that would address infrastructure and agriculture.

People who accept climate change is real and humans have contributed to it are not waiting for the US government to make the first move. Many of the efforts to adapt to climate change in the United States come from local government and private initiatives. For example, Phoenix, Arizona, is protecting its water supply from extreme heat and drought. The city taps its groundwater reserves only during periods of extended drought and instead relies primarily on renewable surface water. A number of private companies manufacture and install solar panels on residences and commercial buildings. People are taking the initiative and adapting to the climate changes they see in their own backyards.

CAFE STANDARDS: IMPROVING FUEL ECONOMY

Corporate Average Fuel Economy, or CAFE, standards were established in 1975 to increase the fuel economy of light trucks and cars as a way to save fuel costs and reduce oil use. President George W. Bush strengthened the standards in December 2007. President Obama followed suit in 2012, raising the CAFE fuel economy standards to 54.5 miles per gallon (23.1 km/L) for cars and light trucks by 2025.[16]

CHAPTER
FIVE

FUELING
THE FUTURE

The burning of fossil fuels for energy, transportation, and industrial, residential, and commercial uses accounts for nearly all the carbon dioxide emissions in the United States. Since people all over the world rely on fossil fuels for energy and transportation, it is improbable society will completely eliminate its use of oil, coal, and natural gas. Instead, humans will need to find ways to stop greenhouse gases from affecting the atmosphere, or adapt to the changes they cause. Scientists are developing various solutions to these problems, including capturing carbon dioxide from the air, integrating renewable energy into energy resources, and developing ways to improve current infrastructure to make it more efficient and capable of handling increased demand due to rising temperatures.

In addition to their effects on climate change, fossil fuels also contribute to air pollution, which has serious impacts on human health.

Addicted to Fossil Fuels

Whether they use them to heat their homes, light up their rooms, drive their cars, or power their schools, people around the world are addicted to cheap energy from fossil fuels. Oil alone accounts for approximately 40 percent of global carbon dioxide emissions.[1] Though the United States was using less oil in 2014 than it had in the last few decades, worldwide use is still increasing due to growing demand in developing nations such as China and India. As people continue relying on oil for fuel, companies and governments will need to tap unconventional sources, such as the oil sands in Alberta, Canada, or shale oil in the Bakken formation of North Dakota. Methods for extracting oil from these sources often release toxic chemicals into the air, land, and water.

Coal has similar problems. China is the world's largest

GREENHOUSE GAS EMISSIONS

In 2010, 65 percent of greenhouse gases released into the atmosphere across the world were from the burning of fossil fuels. The rest were released directly through agriculture, waste, or deforestation.

More than one-quarter of the greenhouse gases emitted in 2010 came from industry use, while another 15 percent came from burning fuel for transportation. Energy needs account for approximately 13 percent of global greenhouse gas emissions.[2]

user of coal, and the country has tripled its use of the substance in the last ten years. The United States is a close second. In 2012, coal supplied approximately 37 percent of electricity in the United States.[3] The resource meets 30 percent of the world's energy needs.[4] Though coal is a popular source of energy, its drawbacks affect public health and the environment. The air that leaves the smokestack at a coal power plant is not very clean. Toxic smog from coal plants causes respiratory problems, including asthma. In China, the smog in large cities periodically gets so bad visibility decreases

NEW PLACES TO FIND OIL

Demand for oil remains strong in both developed and developing nations. As easily accessible supplies run out, the oil industry has had to get creative with where and how it extracts the resource. In the United States, companies use a procedure known as hydraulic fracturing, or fracking, to extract oil and natural gas in shale formations in North Dakota, Montana, and Texas. They also mine oil shale formations that cover terrain in Tennessee, Kentucky, Indiana, Ohio, Michigan, Colorado, Wyoming, and Utah.

Internationally, companies drill for oil on huge offshore rigs off the coast of Brazil, as well as in the oil sands of Alberta, Canada. Climate change has made the oil in the Arctic available for drilling. Warmer temperatures have caused glaciers in the region to recede, giving oil companies access to the oil below. These new sources will extend the availability of fossil fuels, but they are typically more expensive than traditional sources. They also tend to pollute the surrounding environment, including the drinking water supply.

and poor air quality forces students to stay home from school. In 2010, the World Health Organization Global Burden of Disease estimated 1.2 million people died in China as a result of air pollution.[5]

Scientists are developing ways to change how the world consumes energy so greenhouse gas emissions are taken into account. Some of these technologies, such as direct air capture and renewable energy technology,

CAN WE CLEAN COAL?

In recent years, the US Department of Energy has made efforts to develop technology to "clean" coal by capturing the carbon dioxide from power plant emissions before the gas even makes it to the atmosphere. The Department of Energy has proposed renovating existing coal power plants so they can capture carbon dioxide and then store it, possibly by burial. Proponents of clean coal technologies believe retrofitting carbon capture systems will help reduce atmospheric carbon dioxide levels and make coal-fired power plants more efficient.

However, clean coal efforts have their critics. One problem is that it is difficult to store carbon dioxide once it is captured. There is no guarantee carbon dioxide will stay underground once buried. In addition, implementing clean coal technology requires more coal to produce the same amount of energy than a conventional coal power plant does. Companies would need to mine and transport more raw materials, which is harmful to the environment. Using more coal also means more toxic by-products, such as fly ash, would be released into the environment.

are on the cutting edge, while others, such as increasing energy efficiency, have been around for decades.

Capturing Carbon

Researchers recognize people are not going to completely stop using fossil fuels for energy overnight. To curb the effects of energy use, some companies are researching ways to capture and store the carbon dioxide emitted from burning fossil fuels.

Coal- and natural gas–fired power plants are adopting methods that allow them to capture carbon dioxide as it leaves their smokestacks. Approximately 120 facilities in the United States use carbon capture technology. After the carbon dioxide is captured, it is transported in a pipeline to an underground storage site. Usually, these sites are in coal beds and old oil fields. Experts project the United States could store between 2,000 and 22,000 short tons (1,800 and 20,000 billion metric tons) of carbon dioxide.[6]

Though often vilified, carbon dioxide is actually a useful by-product. Many industries, including companies that make carbonated drinks and those that grow algae, use carbon dioxide in the manufacturing process. In the future, carbon that is stored underground may be put

The Schwarze Pumpe power plant in Germany is piloting carbon capture storage technology.

to use. Companies may go into the carbon capturing business to supply other industries and make a profit.

Researchers are working on a new technology that may help reduce the level of carbon dioxide in the atmosphere. Direct air capture would "catch" carbon dioxide in the air and then store it somewhere other than the atmosphere, generally underground. The technology would capture carbon from the air only after concentrations go over a certain threshold. Though carbon dioxide levels in the atmosphere would remain high, capturing carbon would keep concentrations at safe levels without requiring society to reduce its use of fossil fuels.

When fossil fuel power plants emit greenhouse gases, the atmosphere carries them away and distributes them worldwide. Direct air capture would make it possible to capture carbon from anywhere on Earth, regardless of where it originated. For example, it would be possible to capture carbon dioxide released in China halfway across the world in Brazil. Direct air carbon capture would work well for trapping and storing carbon dioxide from moving vehicles.

However, direct air capture of carbon dioxide is likely to be very expensive if implemented. Experts estimate the cost to remove just 1.1 short tons (1 metric ton) of carbon dioxide from the atmosphere could be $600 to $1,000. The typical American produces 22 short tons (20 metric tons) of carbon dioxide every year, which means capturing the carbon dioxide of just one American could cost $12,000 to $20,000 a year.[7] While installing carbon capture technology may be an effective way to compensate for high greenhouse gas concentrations in the future, it is not an easy fix.

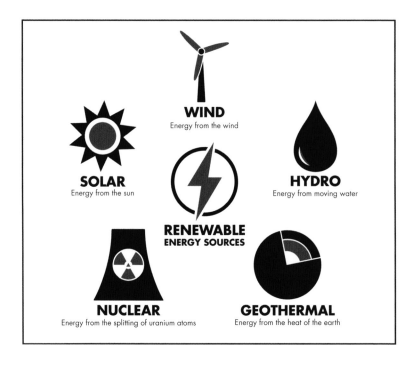

WIND
Energy from the wind

SOLAR
Energy from the sun

HYDRO
Energy from moving water

RENEWABLE
ENERGY SOURCES

NUCLEAR
Energy from the splitting of uranium atoms

GEOTHERMAL
Energy from the heat of the earth

Relying on Renewable Resources

While direct air capture of carbon dioxide may be
years away, people around the world today are taking
advantage of renewable resources to supplement their
fossil fuel use. Renewable resources produce energy but
do not emit greenhouse gases. Examples include wind,
solar, geothermal, and hydropower. Nuclear power is
another common alternative to fossil fuels and does not
emit greenhouse gases, but it creates other issues.

Supplementing fossil fuel energy with renewable
energy can help society keep atmospheric carbon dioxide
levels within safe thresholds. It also helps secure the

energy supply. Since wind and solar power are locally available sources of energy, countries such as the United States could rely less on foreign sources of energy, such as oil from the Middle East, or expensive and hazardous new sources such as oil sands and offshore drilling in the Arctic. However, to incorporate more renewable resources into the US energy system, the country would need to invest in more infrastructure to account for fluctuations in wind and sunshine. One solution would be to develop storage technologies and facilities so the nation's power grid is not threatened by a period of decreased wind or solar energy.

CONTROVERSIAL NUCLEAR ENERGY

Discussion of alternatives to fossil fuels often includes expanding the use of nuclear energy. However, there is a lot of controversy surrounding nuclear power. Though nuclear energy does not produce greenhouse gases, nuclear fuel is highly radioactive and can cause catastrophic damage in the event of an accident. Storing spent fuel and managing leakages present huge challenges as well.

However, expanding the use of nuclear energy would provide some benefits. In addition to producing no greenhouse gases, nuclear energy may eventually be a viable replacement for fossil fuels. Most renewable energy sources struggle to meet the energy demands fossil fuels can. Nuclear power may provide a way to greatly reduce greenhouse gas emissions from the burning of fossil fuels for energy.

Improving Energy Infrastructure

Another way society may adapt its habits and behaviors to climate change is to make the infrastructure that generates and distributes energy more efficient. A group of researchers with the Alliance to Save Energy, a nonprofit organization of business, environmental, and government leaders, has ideas for how governments can make electric and water infrastructures more efficient and secure when extreme weather, heat waves, and other climate change impacts make larger demands on national infrastructure.

Making energy systems more efficient helps preserve and even extend the usefulness of energy resources. This is an important adaptation for a changing climate, when extreme heat or drought may strain a city's ability to meet residents' energy and water needs. When regions experience heat waves, people use air conditioning more, straining energy resources. Requiring residents to install smart energy meters and programmable thermostats can help cities allocate energy more effectively. Similarly, governments can protect water resources by finding and repairing leaks in a timely manner, upgrading equipment and maintenance policies

Experts continue seeking ways to make energy transmission more efficient than standard power lines.

to improve energy efficiency, and adopting a water conservation policy. Upgrading and renovating current energy infrastructure will help cities and regions continue meeting energy and water demands as the planet becomes warmer.

CHAPTER
SIX

CHANGING OCEANS

O ceans are vast ecosystems, covering more than 70 percent of Earth's surface.[1] Climate change is altering Earth's oceans in numerous ways that affect humans. Warmer water temperatures affect sea levels and weather patterns all over the world. Increased concentrations of carbon dioxide in the oceans are killing off marine species that provide the backbone of ocean ecosystems. These species are also crucial food and income sources for people across the globe. As the oceans suffer from the effects of climate change, humans will need to adapt.

Our Changing Oceans

Earth's atmosphere and the oceans have a close relationship. They exchange energy, water, and even chemicals, including gases. Earth's oceans hold between one-fifth and one-third of the planet's carbon dioxide,

Coral reef ecosystems are sensitive to changes in ocean temperature and acidity.

absorbing excess carbon dioxide from the atmosphere. While this can help slow the rise of atmospheric carbon dioxide levels, elevated carbon dioxide levels in the oceans may spell disaster for the plants and animals that live there.

Greenhouse gases and global warming have another effect on the planet's oceans. Rising global temperatures cause an increase in the surface temperatures of the world's oceans. Water expands as it warms, so warmer oceans contribute to a rise in sea levels. Warmer air and water temperatures can cause the vast glaciers at the poles to melt into the ocean, resulting in rising sea levels. Higher sea levels can cause damage to the property of people who live along the coasts, on islands, or in other low-lying areas as water levels encroach on land and cause erosion. They also change the coastal ecosystems, changing marshes into open ocean and causing freshwater sources to become saltier as sea levels rise.

Earth's oceans absorb 80 to 90 percent of the extra heat trapped by the greenhouse effect.[2] The heat is initially stored in the surface water of the oceans, but eventually it moves down to the deeper parts of the oceans, increasing the global average temperature

Coastal erosion coupled with the highest tidal surge in 60 years left this Norfolk, England, home overhanging a sea cliff.

of seawater. Since 1955, ocean temperatures have experienced a warming trend, with steeper increases in temperatures in the years after 1990.

All this warming has a profound impact across the globe. Warmer water temperature leads to a loss of nutrients in the sea, which makes it more difficult for marine species to survive. It also destroys marine habitats. Most fish have a preferred water temperature. Warming oceans may push cold-water fish farther north or lead to declining populations.

Warming oceans also lead to more extreme weather. When the oceans store heat, storm systems can use that heat as energy, creating stronger storms. Humans will need to find ways to adapt to these changes as the planet warms.

Melting Glaciers

One consequence of warmer ocean temperatures—and warmer global temperatures—is melting glaciers. A glacier is a large mass made of ice and snow that has built up over a number of years. Glaciers are present year-round and move very slowly over the landscape on which they rest. They also contain more than two-thirds of the world's freshwater.[3] Many glaciers around the world have been shrinking since the 1970s, but data from some glaciers indicate they have been losing mass since the 1940s.

It is normal for glaciers to lose and gain mass over time. While melting and ice calving shrink glaciers, in normal conditions that mass is regained as new snow accumulates on the glacier. However, in the last few decades, glaciers have been doing more melting than growing due to rising global temperatures. When glaciers melt, the freshwater trapped in the glacier flows into the sea. This means potential drinking water supplies are being lost to the undrinkable ocean. This increases the need to adapt infrastructure to protect current freshwater resources. Melting glaciers also contribute to rising sea levels.

Rising Sea Levels

Prior to 1900, sea levels experienced very little change throughout human history. However, after the

THE EXTREME ICE SURVEY

It can be difficult to see the effect of climate change on glaciers because of their massive size. In the spring of 2005, environmental photographer James Balog set out to show the world how climate change was affecting glaciers all over the world. The National Geographic Society sent Balog on assignment to document climate change. While in the Arctic, he decided to expand the project into the Extreme Ice Survey.

Balog and his team of researchers set up time-lapse cameras all over the world to document melting glaciers in places including Mount Everest, the Alps, Iceland, Greenland, Canada, the Rockies, and Alaska. The cameras captured the ice moving and melting over a period of months and years. The Extreme Ice Survey cameras use solar power and batteries to continually operate. They are dustproof and waterproof. To install and monitor them, Balog and his team travel up to 80 miles (129 km) from the nearest village on dogsleds, horses, skis, and sometimes even helicopters. Some photos depict glaciers that people have never documented. And since these glaciers are melting, no one will ever see them as they once were.

beginning of the 1900s, sea levels began rising. The long-term average global sea level rise before 1993 was approximately 0.07 inches (0.18 cm) per year. Between 1993 and 2011, however, global sea levels rose between 0.11 and 0.13 inches (0.28 to 0.33 cm) per year, or approximately twice as fast. Though fractions of an inch may not seem like much, these numbers are just averages. Some states along the mid-Atlantic and Gulf coasts in the United States have seen a rise of eight inches (20 cm).[4]

When sea levels rise, beaches and coasts start to flood and erode and marshes disappear. Salt water creeps into freshwater systems, including groundwater. All these consequences affect human infrastructure. Homes along the coast can be swept away, as can electric lines and water and sewage systems. The University of Arizona studied the vulnerabilities of coastal cities with populations of more than 50,000 in the United States. The research found rising sea levels in the 2000s would affect 40.5 million people in these cities. Major cities such as Miami, Tampa, New Orleans, and Virginia Beach may lose up to 10 percent of their land area by the end of the century.[5] Low-lying nations around the world, such as Bangladesh, may be ravaged by rising sea levels. Low-lying islands, such as Kiribati in the Pacific Ocean and the Maldives in the Indian Ocean, may disappear altogether due to rising sea levels and resulting erosion. Rising sea levels reduce the land available for agriculture and for people to live on. They destroy coastal wetlands, making inland areas more vulnerable to flooding.

People, organizations, and governments are now developing ways to adapt to rising seas. During Sandy, rising sea levels contributed to a higher than normal storm surge. Engineers, in hopes of finding solutions for New York harbor, are studying how the Netherlands, a low-lying country that sits along the North Sea, deals with rising sea levels. The Netherlands has built several huge devices, including a long sea wall and enormous

BANGLADESH IN PERIL

Low-lying countries all over the world will need to adapt to climate change, not least of all the South Asian country of Bangladesh. Most of Bangladesh's land lies only meters above sea level, leaving it vulnerable to rising sea levels. Climate models predict that by 2100, a three-foot (1 m) rise in sea level will force more than 30 million Bangladeshis from their homes.[6] In the meantime, salt water could seep into freshwater sources, making drinking water scarce and swamping farmland with seawater. In addition to the perils posed by rising sea levels, Bangladesh is also threatened by cyclones from the Bay of Bengal. As the planet and the oceans warm, these storms could become more extreme.

gates intended to hold back the ocean during storms, so major population centers are not flooded. Some people would like to install a similar system in New York City.

Others are studying ways to add natural barriers, like coastal wetlands and thriving marshlands. Engineers are reconstructing beaches around the world to reduce erosion and increase tourism. Communities can allow beaches to erode and flood naturally while encouraging salt marshes and wetlands to thrive. In New York harbor, scientists are looking at how marine species such as blue mussels can help the harbor adapt to the effects of sea level rise. Mussel beds and the coastal marshes they help create may absorb some of the energy from higher storm surge levels in the future.

Adapting to Acidic Oceans

Oceans absorb carbon dioxide from the air to stay in balance with the concentration of carbon dioxide in the atmosphere. In the last 250 years, that balance has been disrupted. Oceans have absorbed 40 percent of the carbon dioxide humans produce.[7] That is approximately 550 billion short tons (500 billion metric tons) of carbon dioxide.[8] All that carbon dioxide has serious consequences for ocean ecosystems. Carbon dioxide also lowers the pH level of the oceans, making them more acidic. When carbon dioxide reacts with seawater, it produces the chemical compound carbonic acid. When there is too much carbonic acid in the water, it makes the water acidic and dissolves the calcium carbonate that corals, plankton, and shellfish rely on to produce their hard shells and skeletons. That means shellfish develop weak and brittle shells. Acidic oceans also stunt shellfish growth and increase death rates in shellfish populations. The acidification of the oceans makes it difficult for corals to reproduce. When corals cannot reproduce, coral populations decrease, affecting the rest of the ecosystem, including fish and shellfish.

Though ocean acidification directly affects small animals, its impact runs up the food chain to humans.

OCEAN PH

Without outside interference, ocean pH levels remain fairly consistent—so consistent, in fact, that until the Industrial Revolution, there was no significant change in the ocean's pH level for at least 800,000 years. Since the Industrial Revolution, however, the ocean has had to absorb more carbon dioxide due to humans burning fossil fuels. As a result, the ocean has acidified by 30 percent since the 1750s, even though the pH balance has changed just slightly. Scientists project that by 2100, the ocean could acidify by 100 percent.[9] Such rapid and dramatic change could have a profoundly negative impact on marine life, including coral reefs and shellfish.

People rely on the sea for food as well as their livelihoods.

Approximately one in six people—more than 1 billion humans—on the planet rely on the ocean as their primary food source.[10] Decreasing fish populations may mean increased malnutrition and hunger.

To adapt to more acidic oceans, some shellfish larvae growers in the Pacific Northwest are changing their habits. They only pump fresh seawater into their shellfish beds on days where acidity levels are lower. They also add eel grass and sodium carbonate to raise the pH level of the seawater, reducing acidity.

Another way to adapt to increasing carbon dioxide in seawater is to plant more marine marsh plants such as mangrove trees and sea grass. Just as trees and plants on land absorb carbon dioxide from the air, marine plants soak up and store carbon dioxide from the oceans. Though this adaptation would not be possible in deep water, it can help reduce ocean acidity locally. It may also help improve the health of coral reefs, since carbon dioxide–absorbing sea grass tends to grow near coral reefs. The sea grass would absorb the carbon dioxide that contributes to acidification and coral reef troubles.

LOSING FISH HABITAT

Corals are not the only creatures losing out to climate change. All the plants and animals that call corals home also suffer. Warmer ocean waters eradicate the algae that give corals their color, known as bleaching. If ocean acidification continues killing off coral, lots of fish will lose their habitats, an alarming notion given that a quarter of all known fish species spend at least part of their lives in coral reefs. Other animals, from tiny snails to manatees and sea turtles, also call coral reefs home. Losing coral reefs puts all these animals in peril.

CHAPTER
SEVEN

HEAT, DROUGHTS, AND FLOODS

Global temperature rise can affect weather events of all sorts. Some changes are gradual, potentially leading to an increase in heat-related diseases and the migration of human populations. When the global average temperature is warmer, regions may experience hotter individual days and heat waves that last longer or occur more frequently, leading to more deaths from heatstroke and other heat-related illnesses. It also allows tropical diseases, such as malaria, to extend their reach into areas that were formerly too cool for the disease to take hold. Warmer temperatures also contribute to high air pollution levels. Air pollution can cause respiratory illnesses such as asthma to become more severe. Young children, the elderly, and those who work outside are at particular risk.

Warmer temperatures may also lead to people migrating from their homes. International organizations

Drought in already dry regions can lead to food shortages, as happened in Senegal and neighboring countries in 2011 to 2012.

71

estimate climate change will provoke 200 to 700 million people to migrate by 2050.[1] For example, people who live in the Arctic may encounter melting permafrost and less sea ice, requiring them to migrate north, if possible, or adapt their ways of life to the changes. Populations along the equator or in deserts, on the other hand, may move to escape drier, hotter conditions. Extreme weather events such as hurricanes, droughts, and floods also cause people to migrate.

These types of events are likely to get worse. Rising global temperatures can cause droughts and floods to increase in severity. Indeed, countries all over the world are already experiencing extreme droughts and severe flooding. The events have an impact on public health, infrastructure, and food security. As droughts and flooding become more severe, humans will need to find ways to adapt to excess water—or the lack of it. Changes to farming practices, upgrades to sewage systems and flood maps, and city planning can help society adapt to extreme drought and flood.

Devastating Droughts

The American Meteorological Society defines drought as a "period of abnormally dry weather sufficiently

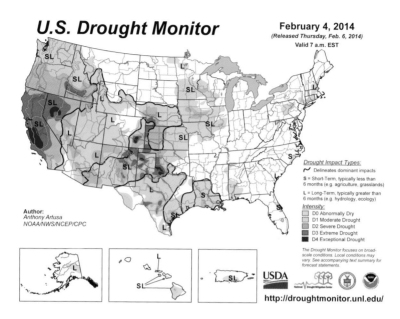

U.S. Drought Monitor

February 4, 2014
(Released Thursday, Feb. 6, 2014)
Valid 7 a.m. EST

Author:
Anthony Artusa
NOAA/NWS/NCEP/CPC

Drought Impact Types:
~ Delineates dominant impacts
S = Short-Term, typically less than
6 months (e.g. agriculture, grasslands)
L = Long-Term, typically greater than
6 months (e.g. hydrology, ecology)

Intensity:
D0 Abnormally Dry
D1 Moderate Drought
D2 Severe Drought
D3 Extreme Drought
D4 Exceptional Drought

The Drought Monitor focuses on broad-
scale conditions. Local conditions may
vary. See accompanying text summary for
forecast statements.

USDA

http://droughtmonitor.unl.edu/

Much of the country was drier than average at the beginning of 2014.

long enough to cause a serious . . . imbalance" between surface, atmospheric, and underground water systems.[2] A lack of precipitation can cause serious water shortages. Drought has many impacts on the well-being of humans, including reduction in crop yields and decreased water supply. Scientists are working on ways to adapt to drier conditions, including development of drought-resistant crops and better management of drinking water.

Climate change scientists project rising global temperatures will cause the distribution of rainfall to shift. That means some places that are arid may experience more rainfall, while others will get even less rainfall than they currently do. These changes will have an impact on populations in dry areas such as deserts and in countries that produce much of the world's food, such as the United States, Ukraine, and Kazakhstan.

At any given time in the years between 2000 and 2012, 30 to 70 percent of the land in the United States was experiencing abnormally dry conditions. The year 2012 was one of the driest years on record across the globe. Between July and December, more than half of the United States was under drought conditions.

105 DEGREES AND CLIMBING

During the 2012 drought that fell across the Midwest United States, the country also experienced extreme heat. In fact, 2012 is the warmest year on record for the United States. The drought was likely the result of a Pacific Ocean weather system that in the past affected the United States every few decades but now comes every few years.

In Asia in 2013, extreme heat broke several city records. Shanghai, China, hit 105.4 degrees Fahrenheit (40.8°C) in August, the highest since the city began keeping records

in 1873. Similarly, Shimanto, Japan, reached 105.8 degrees Fahrenheit (41°C), a record for that city.[3] Climate change scientists currently project heat waves will become more frequent as global temperature rises. One study conducted by researchers at two European institutes predicts instances of the most severe type of heat waves will increase by 2100. Extreme heat has several negative impacts on society. Heatstroke puts the lives of many people at risk, and countries' electric grids are strained when millions of people try to crank up their air conditioning units.

The Midwest was particularly affected, suffering the worst period of drought in 56 years.[4] Across the ocean, countries such as Ukraine, Pakistan, and Kazakhstan all experienced drought conditions. Compounding the effects of drought was a weak monsoon season that was shorter than usual. The 2012 droughts had a negative impact on food supplies around the world. Prices for crops such as corn, wheat, and soybeans all went up because there was less supply due to lack of rainfall. Climate change scientists predict rice yields in the world's poorest countries will not keep pace with the demand. Experts are developing ways to increase yields to meet the needs of the world's population, including drought-resistant varieties.

Adapting to the effects of drought is a primary concern of the agricultural industry, including farmers and companies that supply seed and other farm supplies. In Africa, scientists predict rainfall patterns will change as Earth warms, but they are unsure how. Farmers will need to adopt a variety of practices to adapt to unpredictable rainfall. One such practice is the use of cover crops, or plants farmers use to improve soil quality and reduce erosion. Another method is no-till sowing, which allows farmers to plant seeds without turning the soil. Both help retain moisture in the soil, helping farmers continue to grow crops in dry weather. Some soil experts expect employing these methods may help soil keep up to 85 percent of the precipitation that falls on cropland. Currently, that number is only 50 percent.[5] Some farmers may opt to plant corn that has been bred or genetically modified to be drought-resistant. Some seed companies, such as Monsanto, have already started developing and selling such seeds. However, there is no guarantee modified seeds or other adaptations will work or be needed due to the unpredictability of future extreme weather.

Ferocious Floods

Just as it is expected to increase the severity of drought, climate change is predicted to cause more extreme flooding across the globe. A warmer global temperature allows the atmosphere to hold more moisture, so when storms develop, they are able to release more precipitation. In the summer of 2007, for example, the United Kingdom experienced rainfall exceeding any recorded since 1879 by 20 percent.[6] On July 2, 2011, Copenhagen, Denmark, got six inches (15 cm) of rain in less than three hours, flooding roads and cellars and costing more than $1 billion in damage.[7]

Flooding causes a variety of problems for humans, from disrupting daily lives to displacing flood refugees. When floodwaters encroach on cities and towns, they can contaminate drinking water and overwhelm sewage systems, allowing contents to spill over. As Mike McDonald found during Sandy, flooding can also put people at risk for injury and death.

COPENHAGEN'S CLIMATE ADAPTATION PLAN

On July 2, 2011, Copenhagen received six inches (15 cm) of rain in less than three hours. Cellars and roads were flooded, and damage from the rain cost the city more than $1 billion.[8] The event shocked the city into making major changes, outlined in the citywide Climate Adaptation Plan.

The plan outlines three levels of adaptation: prevent damage, minimize damage, and reduce vulnerability. Where the risk of damage is high, the city will work to prevent the damage from happening in the first place by building on higher ground, constructing dikes, and expanding sewers to accommodate more rainwater. In places where it is not feasible to prevent damage, Copenhagen hopes to minimize loses with waterproof cellars, warning systems for severe rainfalls, and creative ways to store rainfall until it can be drained. The city is working to reduce vulnerability in a number of ways, including building new pumping stations, replacing concrete with grass and trees in parks, and redirecting floodwaters from roads and cellars to parking lots, parks, and sports fields, where it will do less damage. Copenhagen hopes these adaptations will make it less vulnerable to flooding in the future.

There are several actions humans can take to adapt to more extreme flooding. Updating infrastructure can help protect drinking water, while implementing evacuation plans can help manage people displaced by flooding. After Sandy, for example, the state of New York created a plan to adopt new flood insurance maps that take into account rising sea levels so people can evaluate the risk of living near the coast. The state is also planning updates to infrastructure.

In other cases, people may move away from low-lying areas so their homes will be in less danger of flooding. Investing in this type of relocation may be more feasible for developed countries that have the resources to move people around. However, developing countries, which often have housing that can be easily swept away by floodwaters, may lack the resources to relocate their citizens. Another adaptation would be to replant trees on cleared lands, since trees help forest soils soak up more water than bare spaces and help hold the land together. Wetlands accomplish a similar goal.

Floods that follow droughts can be more severe because the parched earth can't absorb water quickly enough.

Food Security in Extreme Drought or Flooding

Rising temperatures, drought, and flooding pose grave risks to food security all over the world. Over the next 20 years, demand for food around the globe is expected to rise 50 percent, even as extreme drought and flooding are expected to increase.[9] Predicting how droughts and floods may affect a particular place in a particular year is tricky. Yet food security experts believe there are many opportunities to adapt farming methods to improve

RE-GREENING IN NIGER

One re-greening success story is taking place in the West African country of Niger. Since 1975, farmers in the regions of Maradi and Zinder have planted trees on 12.5 million acres (5.1 million ha) of farmland.[10] Researchers who looked at the effects of the plantings found they improved soil quality and crop yields, increasing the food security of the farmers and surrounding communities. This in turn helped reduce hunger and poverty as well as conflict between farmers.

the state of food security, even in some of the world's most vulnerable regions.

Encouraging the growth of trees on farmland is a promising way for farmers to keep their crops thriving in dry periods. This is called farmer-managed natural regeneration or re-greening. Re-greening is a way for farmers to reclaim land that is in danger of turning into desert. All farmers need to do is encourage the growth of plants with woody stems and trunks on their farms. These practices lead to reduced temperatures and wind speed due to the trees' foliage. This practice also contributes to lower levels of carbon dioxide in the atmosphere, since the plants are absorbing the gas. More trees also lead to more fertile soil, yielding more crops and, as a result, more food security.

Using sustainable farming techniques is another way to adapt to climate change. Conventional farming encourages farmers to plant a lot of a single crop, which requires the use of fertilizers made from fossil fuels. Sustainable farming, on the other hand, encourages farmers to employ several different techniques to increase yields while developing healthy soils that retain moisture. Practices such as planting cover crops, crop rotation, and even warding off disease and pests with beneficial insects are all examples of sustainable farming. Sustainable farming can help during periods of drought and flooding.

In the summer of 2008, the midwestern United States experienced rainfall that flooded farmland, costing $15 billion in damage and leaving two dozen people dead.[11] Though many farmers who used conventional methods suffered losses during the storm, Mark Shepard of New Forest Farm near Madison, Wisconsin, had a successful growing season. Shepard was using sustainable farming methods. New Forest Farm grows a variety of crops, including berries, peas, and asparagus, a diversity that helps the soil retain nutrients and moisture. The variety of plants and healthy soil were able to absorb the deluge during summer 2008.

An Indiana farmer plants radishes and rye as a winter cover crop.

The experience at New Forest Farm is not a fluke. Organic farming uses strategies to promote biodiversity and biological activity in the soil. A study of conventional and organic farming over the course of 30 years found organic farming practices used less water and less energy to produce the same amount of crops as conventional farming.[12] Though the study is not peer-reviewed, it is the longest side-by-side comparison of conventional and organic agriculture ever conducted. The CEO of the Rodale Institute, which conducted the study, finds evidence organic farming could reduce US greenhouse gas emissions by one-quarter if 434 million acres (176 million ha) of US farmland were converted to organic farming practices. That would be a reduction of 1.6 billion short tons (1.5 billion metric tons) of carbon dioxide.[13]

Though droughts and flooding are expected to become more extreme over the next several decades, humans have the capacity to adapt to drier—or wetter—conditions. Changes to farming practices and the infrastructure that carries sewage and drinking water can help communities adapt to severe drought and flooding. Adapting agricultural practices will help keep global food supplies secure, even when little rain falls or fields are flooded.

ANIMALS AND EXTREME WEATHER

Animals are not immune to the effects of drought. Just as it puts strain on human water and food resources, drought makes it harder for animals to find food and water supplies. More animals die, and when female mammals do not get enough nutrients, their milk production goes down, which means their offspring suffer or even die. This can decrease the population of a species over the long term.

Flooding poses health and safety risks to animals as well as humans. Floods and heavy precipitation destroy habitats and food sources. In 2012, a British songbird called the blackcap produced 62 percent fewer babies than the species had on average between 2006 and 2011 due to a breeding season hampered by chilly, wet weather.[14]

GLETSCHERSTAND
GLACIERPOSITION
1990

CHAPTER
EIGHT

CAN WE FIX THE FUTURE?

It is difficult to know what climate change adaptations and mitigations may be developed throughout the next century. Adaptations and mitigations must be coupled—society will have to adapt to climate change that is happening while working to mitigate worse future change. A variety of projects are in progress now, and engineers and scientists are testing new ideas all the time.

Smart Meters and Smart Homes

New technology could help mitigate climate change by reducing individuals' home energy use. The electric meters found on the outside of most homes in the United States are products of the 1900s. They only tell customers and utility companies how much electricity a customer is using. The meters cannot tell the utility company if there is a power outage or help the company

The climate is changing rapidly in some parts of the world. The red sign indicates where the glacier used to reach in 1990.

adapt to days where demand is high. Smart meters, on the other hand, establish two-way communication between the home and the utility company. That helps companies adapt to energy demands and can help make power more reliable, since companies are able to see when homes are experiencing outages rather than wait for customers to call in with outage information. Having outage information at their fingertips helps utility companies better manage their resources during storms or other incidents. The US Energy Information Administration estimates approximately 23 percent of Americans had smart meters in 2011.[1]

Though proponents of smart meters assert the devices improve energy efficiency and give customers information on their energy usage, it is still unclear how useful that information may be. There are also concerns about the meters' security. Smart meters use an Internet connection to communicate with the utility companies. Theoretically hackers could attack the connection and wreak havoc on the electric grid. These concerns have slowed the rollout of smart meters throughout the United States.

Thermostats and appliances also benefit from an Internet connection. Smart thermostats raise and lower the temperature of a home by learning the occupants' habits. Some even adjust temperatures to take advantage of the different rates utility companies charge throughout the day. Smart appliances operate in a similar fashion. For example, a smart refrigerator could use data from a smart meter to learn when off-peak energy hours occur, and then run its energy-intensive defrost cycle to take advantage of those hours. Air-conditioning units may run less often during the day to adapt to changing energy demand during heat waves, reducing strain on the electric grid. Smart energy use will help consumers in the future if energy becomes more expensive or less plentiful.

GREEN CONCRETE?

Electric meters, thermostats, and appliances are not the only things getting smarter— and greener. A British start-up company developed a new concrete that could make the home construction process greener. Five percent of the world's carbon dioxide emissions come from the concrete-making process.[2] The new concrete helps offset those emissions. Instead of carbon-rich limestone, the concrete is made with magnesium silicates that absorb carbon dioxide. That means that over its life, the new concrete absorbs more carbon dioxide than it emits, which scientists call being carbon negative.

Innovative Ways to Adapt to Drought

People around the world are looking for ways to reduce the effects of severe drought. In the dry regions of Africa, people dependent on rain for farming are especially vulnerable to dry weather. They have few resources to cope with the effects of drought, leading to famine, disease, malnutrition, and even increased crime. Experts are working on ways to identify who is the most at risk and how to warn people that a drought might occur soon. They are working to help communities become more resilient in the face of drought by pooling community resources and encouraging people to help their neighbors.

In the United States, researchers are applying for federal grants that would help them test different theories on how to best adapt to drought. In 2013, researchers at more than a dozen universities were awarded grants to test a variety of adaptations, including methods for conserving water for crops and livestock, improving soil health, and determining if innovative livestock grazing methods would help ranchers adapt to drought.

The world's largest tidal energy turbine awaited
installation in the North Sea in 2010.

Harnessing Tidal Energy

While many scientists and companies focus on ways to
implement solar and wind power, some are looking to
an ancient, yet innovative, energy source: tides. The
constant ebb and flow of tides make tidal energy a

predictable and consistent energy resource. People have harnessed the energy in tides since the 700s CE, when residents living along the coasts of what are now Spain, France, and Britain used tidal energy to mill grain. They diverted water from an incoming tide into a storage pond, where it accumulated until the tide changed. On its way back out to sea, the water ran through a wheel, powering a grain mill.

Today, engineers are developing ways to use a similar idea as an alternative to fossil fuels. Modern tidal power uses large, damlike structures called barrages to trap incoming tides in a preexisting estuary. The barrages are open at the bottom, where tide turbines extend the length of the barrage, facing the estuary. As high tide nears, large gates within the barrage slide down to contain the water. When the tide changes, the gates lift and the turbines capture the energy in the water as it rushes back out to sea.

There are many places around the world that would be ideal spots for tidal power, including the Pacific Northwest, the coast along the northeastern United States and Canada, and the northwest coast of France. However, the cost and the unpredictable effects damming estuaries may have on marine ecosystems has held back the adoption of tidal power. The world's only modern tidal power plant is in northern France at the mouth of the La Rance River. Though data indicates the La Rance plant has little negative impact on the surrounding environment, studies of other sites may reveal negative impacts. To avoid these estuary concerns, some scientists are looking into ways to harness tidal power in deeper water further from the coast.

Geoengineering: Mitigating Climate Change

Geoengineering is at the cutting edge of climate change mitigation science. Geoengineering projects look at ways to turn back the clock on global warming, for example by carbon dioxide removal (CDR), which is removing carbon dioxide from the atmosphere, or by

LA RANCE TIDAL POWER STATION

The tidal barrage at the La Rance Tidal Power Station is the first—and only—tidal barrage in the world. Since it began operation in 1966, it has produced an average of 600 gigawatt hours each year.[3] That is enough to power 600,000 homes.[4] The flow of tides through the plant is monitored by an operator, as is the weather forecast, so the plant can be programmed more effectively and efficiently. While some species, such as the sand eel, have experienced reduction in numbers, other animal populations, including the sea bass and cuttlefish, have increased since the plant was built. Other animals that live near or use the river are thriving, too. The tidal barrage of the plant also doubles as a highway.

solar radiation management (SRM), which involves reflecting the sun's energy back into space so less heat is trapped by the greenhouse effect. Geoengineering is considered controversial because current research cannot prove how effective it will be nor predict its potential negative effects.

Geoengineering projects are diverse. Some examples of CDR are modeled on plants. Scientists are developing artificial trees that capture and store carbon dioxide. More controversial is an idea to add iron to the oceans. Iron encourages plankton to grow, which in turn would scrub carbon dioxide from the oceans, just as trees do on land. However, scientists do not know what the short- or long-term effects of pumping vast amounts of iron into the ocean would be. Other experts are developing SRM systems to reflect the sun's rays back out into space. Some SRM ideas are simple, such as building a giant mirror or painting road surfaces or the roofs of buildings white. Others are more complex, such as pumping sulfur aerosols into the atmosphere to increase its reflectivity.

Though some scientists think adapting to and mitigating climate change requires bold action, others question the wisdom of trying to alter Earth's systems and atmosphere, since it is impossible to know the full range of negative impacts these actions could have. Advocates of geoengineering say humans have been inadvertently altering Earth's systems since the Industrial Revolution by pumping carbon dioxide into the atmosphere, and they assert deliberate efforts to reverse this earlier geoengineering are no different.

Adapting to climate change may be one of the most challenging endeavors individuals, nations, and the international community encounter in the next 100 years. As the planet continues warming, people will need to adapt their ways of living to include renewable energy sources, accommodate rising sea levels, and

STRATOSHIELD

One innovative way to reflect the sun's energy back into space may turn the atmosphere slightly yellow. StratoShield, a geoengineering product of Intellectual Ventures, would pump 110,000 short tons (100,000 metric tons) of sulfur aerosols into the atmosphere every year. The aerosol particles would help scatter the sunlight in the atmosphere and reflect some of it back out into space. The company asserts that if the sulfur aerosols were pumped into the atmosphere annually for an indefinite amount of time, it could cool the planet. However, there are drawbacks. StratoShield would cost $20 million to implement initially, and then another $10 million per year over the course of the project. In addition, pumping sulfur into the atmosphere would give the sky a yellow hue. The largest drawback to moving forward with such a program, however, is that no one knows what the negative impacts might be of pumping sulfur into the atmosphere.[5]

Hanging laundry to dry is an easy way to save energy.

protect themselves from extreme weather, including droughts, heat, and floods. Doing so will require not only strong minds in the science and engineering community, but political will and financial resources. In the future, public and private efforts may uncover new, innovative ways for humans to adapt to warmer temperatures. Local, national, and international communities will need to come together to work to adapt to the changing climate—and the changing planet.

THINGS YOU CAN DO

Though there are lots of big ideas on how to mitigate or adapt to climate change, changing one's habits and behaviors starts at home.

- Shut off computers: Three-quarters of the electricity computers use is consumed in standby mode. Turn off computers to save energy.

- Open a window or pull on a sweater: Use natural ventilation or extra layers to conserve energy used to cool or heat homes and schools.

- Bring a bag: Say no to plastic bags on shopping trips. Instead, take along a reusable bag. Plastic bags are made with oil, a fossil fuel.

- Plant a tree: Trees absorb carbon dioxide and release oxygen.

- Take the bus or walk: Using public transportation is an energy-efficient way to get around. Walking produces no greenhouse gases and promotes good health.

- Embrace air-drying: Air-drying clothes saves the energy used to operate a dryer and leaves clothes feeling fresh.

- Go vegetarian or vegan: Raising livestock for meat or dairy leaves a heavy carbon footprint. Saying "no thanks" to meat or dairy even once a week can make a difference.

TIMELINE

Late 1700s

Great Britain starts burning coal for energy, marking the beginning of the Industrial Revolution.

1966

The La Rance Tidal Power Station begins operation in Brittany, France.

1970

President Nixon establishes the Environmental Protection Agency on December 2 and signs the Clean Air Act into law on December 31.

1975

Congress passes the first CAFE standards for cars and light trucks.

1975

Farmers in Niger start using the sustainable farming technique called farmer-managed natural regeneration, or re-greening.

1977

President Carter establishes the Department of Energy on October 1.

1979

In February, the First World Climate Conference is held among international organizations including the United Nations Environment Programme and the World Meteorological Organization.

1988

The World Meteorological Organization and United Nations Environment Programme create the Intergovernmental Panel on Climate Change.

TIMELINE

1992
The United States ratifies the United Nations Framework Convention on Climate Change on October 13.

2005
The Kyoto Protocol takes effect on February 16, with 141 nations ratifying its provisions.

2006
Al Gore's climate change documentary, *An Inconvenient Truth,* comes out in May, as does a series of ads disputing the negative effects of carbon dioxide.

2010

NASA reports in January the decade between 2000 and 2009 was the warmest on record.

2011

The US Congress eliminates the House Committee on Global Warming.

2012

Hurricane Sandy makes landfall near Brigantine, New Jersey, on October 29; President Obama raises fuel efficiency standards for cars and light trucks.

ESSENTIAL FACTS

At Issue

- In the next several decades, humans will need to adapt to climate change, including warmer global temperatures, rising sea levels, ocean acidification, and extreme weather.

- Though most scientists agree climate change is occurring and much of it is caused by humans, it has been historically difficult for policy makers to take action to adapt to climate change.

- Warmer oceans contribute to glacial melting and rising sea levels, which will require people who live along the world's coasts to adapt their way of living.

- Climate change scientists predict Earth will experience more extreme droughts, heat waves, and floods throughout the 2000s. These weather events affect the global food supply and public health, and they put strain on city infrastructures.

Critical Dates
1900s
The world begins warming noticeably.

1997
Countries around the world signed the Kyoto Protocol in Kyoto, Japan. By 2013, there would be 192 parties to the protocol, though the United States remained absent.

2010
A January report from NASA asserted the decade between 2000 and 2009 was the warmest ever recorded.

Quote
"Politicians and parts of the public may think climate change is still up for debate, but for nearly every scientist who knows the subject, the case is closed. . . . But just because the basics of climate science have been established doesn't mean we know everything about how fast the planet will warm—and what will happen when it does."—*Bryan Walsh, writer and editor for TIME magazine*

GLOSSARY

adaptation
The effort society makes to adjust to or prepare for climate change.

anthropogenic
Relating to or resulting from human activity.

barrage
A dam placed in water's path to increase the depth of water or redirect it.

climate change
Significant change in climate measurements over a period of time.

estuary
A passage where river currents meet ocean tides.

fly ash
A fine ash created by the burning of coal.

greenhouse gas
A type of gas that traps heat in the atmosphere and causes the greenhouse effect.

hydrofluorocarbon
A gas that contains hydrogen, carbon, and fluorine.

ice calving
The breaking off of large pieces of ice from a glacier.

infrastructure
The foundational system of a city's resources.

mitigation
The effort society makes to reduce or prevent the effects of climate change.

oil sand
A mix of water, sand, minerals, and bitumen, a heavy oil.

oil shale
A type of rock containing oil.

reflectivity
The ability to bounce light back toward its source.

shale oil
A crude oil extracted from oil shale by heating it up.

sustainable farming
A farming system that uses organic, renewable practices such as cover crops, crop rotation, and renewable energy to produce crops.

think tank
An organization that performs research.

ADDITIONAL RESOURCES

Selected Bibliography

"Climate Change 2013: The Physical Science Basis Summary for Policymakers." *Working Group 1 Contribution to the Fifth Assessment Report of the Intergovernmental Panel on Climate Change.* Intergovernmental Panel on Climate Change, Oct. 2013. Web. 16 Dec. 2013.

Fagan, Brian M. *The Attacking Ocean: The Past, Present, and Future of Rising Sea Levels.* New York: Bloomsbury, 2013. Print.

Nierenberg, Danielle, and Brian Halweil. *2011 State of the World: Innovations That Nourish the Planet.* Worldwatch Institute. New York: Norton, 2011. Print.

Walsh, Bryan. *Global Warming: The Causes, the Perils, the Solutions.* New York: Time, 2012. Print.

Further Readings

Bradman, Tony. *Under the Weather: Stories about Climate Change.* London: Frances Lincoln, 2012. Print.

Gore, Al. *An Inconvenient Truth: The Crisis of Global Warming.* New York: Viking, 2007. Print.

Simpson, Kathleen. *Extreme Weather: Science Tackles Global Warming and Climate Change.* Washington, DC: National Geographic, 2008. Print.

Websites

To learn more about Essential Issues, visit **booklinks.abdopublishing.com**. These links are routinely monitored and updated to provide the most current information available.

For More Information

For more information on this subject, contact or visit the following organizations:

United Nations Visitor Center
First Avenue and Forty-Second Street
New York, NY 10017
212-963-7539
http://visit.un.org
The United Nations holds a climate summit every year for world leaders. Visit the headquarters of the United Nations in New York City.

Woods Hole Oceanographic Institution
266 Woods Hole Road
Woods Hole, MA 02543
508-289-2252
http://www.whoi.edu
Visit the Ocean Science Exhibit Center to learn more about ocean science research, or check in at the information office, where staff members are available to answer your questions.

SOURCE NOTES

Chapter 1. Climate Change or Wild Weather?

1. Ken Serrano. "Tales from the Storm: 'I'm Going to Survive.'" *The Daily Journal*. Gannett, 11 Nov. 2012. Web. 19 Feb. 2014.

2. Victoria Cavaliere and Dave Warner. "A Year after Sandy, Many Still Rebuilding Damaged Homes." *Reuters*. Thomson Reuters, 30 Oct. 2013. Web. 19 Feb. 2014.

3. "Hurricane Sandy (Atlantic Ocean)." *NASA*. NASA, 28 Oct. 2013. Web. 19 Feb. 2014.

4. Tim Sharp. "Superstorm Sandy: Facts about the Frankenstorm." *LiveScience*. TechMedia, 27 Nov. 2012. Web. 19 Feb. 2014.

5. Eric S. Blake, et al. "Tropical Cyclone Report: Hurricane Sandy (AL182012) 22–29 October 2012." *National Hurricane Center*. 12 Feb 2013. Web. 19 Feb. 2014. 1.

6. "Service Assessment: Hurricane/Post-Tropical Cyclone Sandy, October 22–29, 2012." *National Weather Service*. National Oceanic and Atmospheric Administration, May 2013. Web. 19 Feb. 2014. iv.

7. Ibid. 1.

8. Ibid. 1.

9. Ibid. iv.

10. "Working Group 1 Contribution to the IPCC Fifth Assessment Report—Climate Change 2013: The Physical Science Basis (First Draft Underlying Scientific-Technical Assessment)." *Intergovernmental Panel on Climate Change*. IPCC, 30 Sept. 2013. Web. 19 Feb. 2014. 67.

11. Jennifer Chu. "Bigger Storms Ahead." *MIT News*. Massachusetts Institute of Technology, 8 July 2013. Web. 19 Feb. 2014.

12. "Twelfth Session of Working Group 1: Approved Summary for Policy Makers." *Intergovernmental Panel on Climate Change*. IPCC, 27 Sept. 2013. Web. 19 Feb. 2014. 9.

13. Brad Plumer. "Yes, Hurricane Sandy Is a Good Reason to Worry about Climate Change." *Wonkblog*. Washington Post, 29 Oct. 2012. Web. 19 Feb. 2014.

14. Mark Fischetti. "Did Climate Change Cause Hurricane Sandy?" *Observations*. Scientific American, 30 Oct. 2012. Web. 14 Oct. 2013.

15. John Cook, et al. "Quantifying the Consensus on Anthropogenic Global Warming in the Scientific Literature." *Environmental Research Letters* 8.2 (2013). *IOPScience*. Web. 19 Feb. 2014.

Chapter 2. The Science of Climate Change

1. "Climate Change: Basic Information." *Climate Change*. US Environmental Protection Agency, n.d. Web. 19 Feb. 2014.

2. "Climate Change Facts: Answers to Common Questions." *Climate Change*. US Environmental Protection Agency, n.d. Web. 19 Feb. 2014.

3. Bryan Walsh. *Global Warming: The Causes, the Perils, the Solutions*. New York: Time, 2012. Print. 9.

4. "Overview of Greenhouse Gases." *Climate Change*. US Environmental Protection Agency, n.d. Web. 19 Feb. 2014.

5. "Climate Change: Basics." *Climate Change*. US Environmental Protection Agency, n.d. Web. 19 Feb. 2014.

6. "Greenhouse Effect." *Encyclopaedia Britannica*. Encyclopaedia Britannica, 2014. Web. 19 Feb. 2014.

7. "Climate Change Indicators in the United States." *Climate Change*. US Environmental Protection Agency, n.d. Web. 19 Feb. 2014.

8. "Climate Change Facts: Answers to Common Questions." *Climate Change*. US Environmental Protection Agency, n.d. Web. 19 Feb. 2014.

Chapter 3. What Does It Mean to Adapt?

1. "Adaptation Overview." *Climate Change*. US Environmental Protection Agency, n.d. Web. 19 Feb. 2014.

2. "Economics of Adaptation to Climate Change." *World Bank*. World Bank, 6 June 2011. Web. 19 Feb. 2014.

3. Fran Sussman, et al. "Climate Change Adaptation Cost in the US: What Do We Know?" *Climate Policy* 14.2 (2014): 4. *Taylor & Francis Online*. Web. 19 Feb. 2014.

4. Ibid. 7.

5. Ibid. 18.

6. Ibid. 19.

Chapter 4. A Bit of Climate Change History

1. "Causes of Climate Change." *World Meteorological Organization*. World Meteorological Organization, n.d. Web. 19 Feb. 2014.

2. "How Does Climate Change Today Compare with Climate Change in the Past?" *Climate Change Information Resources: New York Metropolitan Region*. Trustees of Columbia University in the City of New York, 2004–2005. Web. 19 Feb. 2014.

3. Sarah Childress. "Timeline: The Politics of Climate Change." *Frontline: Climate of Doubt*. PBS, 23 Oct. 2012. Web. 19 Feb. 2014.

4. Dana Fisher. *National Governance and the Global Climate Change Regime*. Lanham, MD: Rowman & Littlefield, 2004. *Google Book Search*. Web. 19 Feb. 2014.

5. Sarah Childress. "Timeline: The Politics of Climate Change." *Frontline: Climate of Doubt*. PBS, 23 Oct. 2012. Web. 19 Feb. 2014.

6. Ibid.

7. "Fewer Americans See Solid Evidence of Global Warming." *Pew Research Center for the People and the Press*. Pew Research Center, 22 Oct. 2009. Web. 19 Feb. 2014.

8. "Modest Rise in Number Saying There Is 'Solid Evidence' of Global Warming." *Pew Research Center for the People and the Press*. Pew Research, 1 Dec. 2011. Web. 19 Feb. 2014.

9. "Climate Change: Key Data Points from Pew Research." *Pew Research Center*. Pew Research Center, 27 Jan. 2014. Web. 19 Feb. 2014.

10. S. Fred Singer, et al. "Climate Change Reconsidered: 2011 Interim Report." *Heartland Institute*. Heartland Institute, 29 Aug. 2011. Web. 19 Feb. 2014.

11. Sarah Childress. "Timeline: The Politics of Climate Change." *Frontline: Climate of Doubt*. PBS, 23 Oct. 2012. Web. 19 Feb. 2014.

12. Ibid.

SOURCE NOTES CONTINUED

13. Bryan Walsh. *Global Warming: The Causes, the Perils, the Solutions.* New York: Time, 2012. Print. 22.

14. Sarah Childress. "Timeline: The Politics of Climate Change." *Frontline: Climate of Doubt.* PBS, 23 Oct. 2012. Web. 19 Feb. 2014.

15. Justin Gillis. "Obama Puts Legacy at Stake with Clean-Air Act." *New York Times.* New York Times, 25 June 2013. Web. 19 Feb. 2014.

16. White House Office of the Press Secretary. "Obama Administration Finalizes Historic 54.5 MPG Fuel Efficiency Standards." *White House.* White House, 28 Aug. 2012. Web. 19 Feb. 2014.

Chapter 5. Fueling the Future

1. Bryan Walsh. *Global Warming: The Causes, the Perils, the Solutions.* New York: Time, 2012. Print. 30.

2. "World GHG Emissions Flow Chart 2010." *Washington Post.* Washington Post, n.d. Web. 19 Feb. 2014.

3. "Frequently Asked Questions: What Is U.S. Electricity Generation by Energy Source?" *U.S. Energy Information Administration.* US EIA, 9 May 2013. Web. 19 Feb. 2014.

4. Bryan Walsh. *Global Warming: The Causes, the Perils, the Solutions.* New York: Time, 2012. Print. 36.

5. Clay Stranger. "China Smog: Can Energy Efficiency Stop 'Airmageddon'?" *Christian Science Monitor.* Christian Science Monitor, 10 Nov. 2013. Web. 19 Feb. 2014.

6. "Carbon Dioxide Capture and Sequestration." *Climate Change.* US Environmental Protection Agency, n.d. Web. 19 Feb. 2014.

7. Bryan Walsh. *Global Warming: The Causes, the Perils, the Solutions.* New York: Time, 2012. Print. 99.

Chapter 6. Changing Oceans

1. "About 96 Percent of Earth's Water Is in the Ocean." *National Ocean Service.* National Oceanic and Atmospheric Administration, n.d. Web. 19 Feb. 2014.

2. "Climate Change Indicators in the United States: Ocean Heat." *Climate Change.* US Environmental Protection Agency, n.d. Web. 19 Feb. 2014.

3. "The World's Water." *The USGS Water Science School.* USGS, 5 Nov. 2013. Web. 19 Feb. 2014.

4. "Climate Change Indicators in the United States: Sea Level." *Climate Change.* US Environmental Protection Agency, n.d. Web. 19 Feb. 2014.

5. Brian M. Fagan. *The Attacking Ocean: The Past, Present, and Future of Rising Sea Levels.* New York: Bloomsbury, 2013. Print. 227–228.

6. Alex Mifflin. "Bangladesh Is Drowning Because of Climate Change." *Huffington Post: Impact Canada.* Huffington Post, 23 Oct. 2013. Web. 19 Feb. 2014.

7. "Climate Change Indicators in the United States: Ocean Acidity." *Climate Change.* US Environmental Protection Agency, n.d. Web. 19 Feb. 2014.

8. Saskia De Melker. "Coral Reefs and Shellfish Battle Acidifying Oceans." *PBS NewsHour.* PBS, 5 Dec. 2012. Web. 19 Feb. 2014.

9. Ibid.

10. "Resources: About Our Oceans." *Ocean Foundation*. Ocean Foundation, n.d. Web. 19 Feb. 2014.

Chapter 7. Heat, Droughts, and Floods

1. Arthur Max, Associated Press Writer. "Report: Warming Could Cause Greatest Human Migration Ever." *ABC News*. ABC, n.d. Web. 19 Feb. 2014.

2. "Drought vs. Aridity." *National Climatic Data Center*. National Oceanic and Atmospheric Administration, n.d. Web. 19 Feb. 2014.

3. Bryan Walsh. "As Northeast Asia Bakes, Climate Scientists Predict More Extreme Heat Waves on the Horizon." *Time*. Time, 15 Aug. 2013. Web. 19 Feb. 2014.

4. Tim Lister. "The Driest Season: Global Drought Causes Major Worries." *CNN World*. CNN, 8 Sept. 2012. Web. 19 Feb. 2014.

5. Rattan Lal, et al. "Adapting Agriculture to Drought and Extreme Events." *Journal of Soil and Water Conservation* 67.6 (Nov/Dec 2012): 165A–166A. *Journal of Soil and Water Conservation Online*. Web. 19 Feb. 2014.

6. "Flooding." *Climate Change from the BBC Weather Centre*. BBC, July 2009. Web. 19 Feb. 2014.

7. Justin Gerdes. "What Copenhagen Can Teach Cities About Adapting to Climate Change." *Forbes*. Forbes, 31 Oct. 2012. Web. 19 Feb. 2014.

8. Ibid.

9. Bureau of Public Affairs. "Global Hunger and Food Security Initiative: Consultation Document." *US Department of State*. US Department of State, 28 Sept. 2009. Web. 19 Feb. 2014.

10. Danielle Nierenberg and Brian Halweil. *2011 State of the World: Innovations That Nourish the Planet*. New York: Norton, 2011. Print. 86–87.

11. Ibid. 93–94.

12. "Our Work: Farming Systems Trial Overview." *Rodale Institute*. Rodale Institute, n.d. Web. 19 Feb. 2014.

13. Danielle Nierenberg and Brian Halweil. *2011 State of the World: Innovations That Nourish the Planet*. New York: Norton, 2011. Print. 94.

14. "Floods and Wet Weather Could Spell Poor Year for Wildlife in 2013." *Telegraph*. Telegraph Media Group, 6 Jan. 2013. Web. 19 Feb. 2014.

Chapter 8. Can We Fix the Future?

1. "Today in Energy: Smart Meter Deployments Continue to Rise." *US Energy Information Administration*. US EIA, 1 Nov. 2012. Web. 19 Feb. 2014.

2. Alok Jha. "Revealed: The Cement That Eats Carbon Dioxide." *Guardian*. Guardian News and Media, 31 Dec. 2008. Web. 19 Feb. 2014.

3. "La Rance Barrage." *Wyre Tidal Energy*. Wyre Tidal Energy, n.d. Web. 19 Feb. 2014.

4. "How Much Land Does It Take to Produce Solar Energy for 1000 Homes?" *SustainableBusiness.com*. SustainableBusiness.com, 12 Aug. 2013. Web. 19 Feb. 2014.

5. Bryan Walsh. *Global Warming: The Causes, the Perils, the Solutions*. New York: Time, 2012. Print. 92.

INDEX

animals, 15, 28, 59, 61, 67–69, 83,
  88, 91
atmosphere, 11, 17, 18–23, 25,
  35, 36, 41, 47, 48, 50, 52–53,
  59–60, 66, 76, 80, 91–93

Balog, James, 63
Bangladesh, 64–65
Bush, George H. W., 38
Bush, George W., 39, 45

carbon dioxide, 19–20, 22–23, 25,
  28, 36, 41, 47, 48, 50, 51–54,
  59–60, 66–67, 69, 80, 83, 87,
  91–93, 95
carbon dioxide removal, 91–92
Carter, Jimmy, 37
Clean Air Act, 44
Clinton, Bill, 38
coal, 20, 22, 36, 47, 48–51
coastal areas, 7, 9, 21, 26–27, 32,
  60, 64–66, 78, 90–91
Con Edison, 27
concrete, 76, 87
Copenhagen, 77
coral, 67, 69
Corporate Average Fuel Economy,
  45

Department of Energy, 37, 50
direct air carbon capture, 50,
  52–54
drought, 21, 26, 45, 56, 72, 73–76,
  79, 81, 83, 88, 95

economics, 9, 10, 30, 32, 53, 77,
  81, 93
ecosystems, 42, 59, 60, 66–67, 90
Emanuel, Kerry, 12–13
emissions, 20, 22, 25, 38–39, 44,
  47, 48, 50, 51, 53–55, 83, 87
Environmental Protection Agency,
  17, 37
Extreme Ice Survey, 63

fish, 61, 67–69, 91
floods, 7–8, 10, 21, 26, 27–28,
  64–66, 72, 76–79, 81, 83, 95
food security, 21, 26, 33, 59, 68,
  72, 74–75, 79–80
fossil fuels, 22–23, 47, 48, 49, 51,
  53, 54–55, 67, 81, 90, 95

geoengineering, 91–93
glacial ice, 13, 21, 49, 60, 62–63
Global Climate Science Team, 40
Gore, Al, 39
greenhouse effect, 19, 21, 60, 92
greenhouse gases, 17, 18–21, 22,
  25, 35, 36, 38–39, 42, 44, 47,
  48, 50, 53, 54, 55, 60, 83, 95

health, 14, 32, 49–50, 72, 83, 88,
  95
Heartland Institute, 41–42
hurricane, 9, 11–12, 72

Inconvenient Truth, An, 39, 40–41
Industrial Revolution, 22, 36, 40, 67, 93
Intergovernmental Panel on Climate Change, 12–13, 38–39

Katrina (hurricane), 9
Kyoto Protocol, 38–39, 40

La Rance Tidal Power Station, 91

McDonald, Mike, 7–8, 77
migration, 15, 28, 71–72
mitigation, 14, 25, 26, 85, 91, 92, 95
Montreal Protocol, 37–38

National Academy of Sciences, 42
National Weather Service, 9
natural gas, 20, 47, 49, 51
New Jersey, 7, 9, 10–11, 27
New York, 9, 10, 27, 65–66, 78
Nixon, Richard, 37, 44
nuclear power, 37, 54, 55

Obama, Barack, 11, 43–44, 45
ocean acidity, 66–69
ocean temperatures, 11, 13, 59, 60–62, 69
oil, 20, 22, 40, 45, 47, 48, 49, 51, 55, 95
organic farming, 82–83

pollution, 37, 41, 49, 50, 71
public opinion, 40–45

Raymond, Lee, 40
Reagan, Ronald, 37
reflectivity, 18–19, 92, 93
re-greening, 80
renewable energy, 37, 47, 50, 54–55, 93
renewable resources, 54–55
Romney, Mitt, 43–44

Sandy (post-tropical cyclone), 7–11, 13, 14, 27–28, 33, 41, 65, 77–78
sea level, 9–10, 13, 14–15, 21, 23, 26, 32, 59–60, 63–66, 78, 93
Shepard, Mark, 81
smart houses, 56, 85–87
soil, 18, 75–76, 78, 80–82, 88
solar energy, 45, 54–55, 89
solar radiation management, 92
storm surge, 7, 9–10, 13, 65, 66
StratoShield, 93
sustainable farming, 80–81

tides, 7, 10, 13, 89–91

United Nations Environment Programme, 38
Utech, Dan, 44–45

wind energy, 54–55, 89
World Bank, 30
World Health Organization, 50
World Meteorological Organization, 38

ABOUT THE AUTHOR

Amanda Lanser is a freelance writer who lives in Minneapolis, Minnesota. She and her husband are animal lovers and have two cats, Quigley and Aveh, and a greyhound, Laila. Amanda enjoys writing books for kids of all ages as well as learning and writing about climate change.